DK

LANGUAGE ARTS MADE EASY

K Workbook

10 Minutes A Day

Phonics

Consultant Linda Ruggieri

10-minute challenge

Try to complete the exercises for each topic in 10 minutes or less. Note the time it takes you in the "Time taken" column below.

Penguin Random House

DK London
Editor Elizabeth Blakemore
Senior Editor Deborah Lock
US Editor Nancy Ellwood
US Consultant Linda Ruggieri
Managing Editor Christine Stroyan
Managing Art Editor Anna Hall
Senior Production Editor Andy Hilliard
Senior Production Controller Jude Crozier
Jacket Design Development Manager Sophia MTT
Publisher Andrew Macintyre
Associate Publishing Director Liz Wheeler
Art Director Karen Self
Publishing Director Jonathan Metcalf

DK Delhi
Project Editor Neha Ruth Samuel
Senior Art Editor Stuti Tiwari Bhatia
Editorial team Rohini Deb, Manjari Thakur
Assistant Art Editor Radhika Kapoor
Managing Editors Soma B. Chowdhury, Kingshuk Goshal
Managing Art Editor Govind Mittal
Design Consultant Shefali Upadhyay
Senior DTP Designer Tarun Sharma
DTP Designers Anita Yadav, Rakesh Kumar, Harish Aggarwal
Senior Jacket Designer Suhita Dharamjit
Jackets Editorial Coordinator Priyanka Sharma

This American Edition, 2020
First American Edition, 2014
Published in the United States by DK Publishing,
a division of Penguin Random House LLC
1745 Broadway, 20th Floor, New York, NY 10019

Copyright © 2014, 2020 Dorling Kindersley Limited
24 25 10 9 8 7 6 5
005–322739–May/2020

A catalog record for this book
is available from the Library of Congress.
ISBN 978-0-7440-3143-0

DK books are available at special discounts when purchased in bulk for sales promotions, premiums, fund-raising, or educational use. For details, contact: DK Publishing Special Markets, 1745 Broadway, 20th Floor, New York, NY 10019
SpecialSales@dk.com

Printed and bound in China

All images © Dorling Kindersley Limited

www.dk.com

Contents

Time Taken

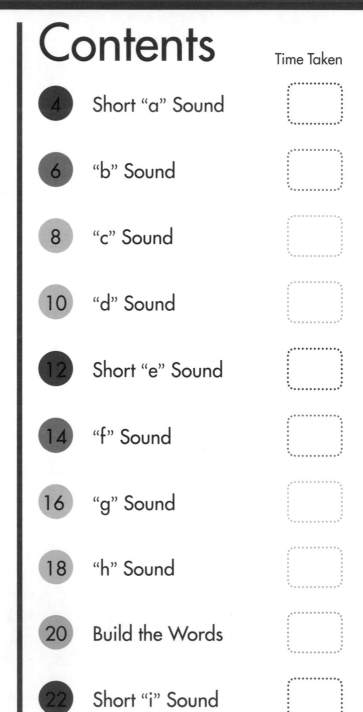

Short "a" Sound

The "a" sound can start words like **a**nt. It can also be in the middle of words like b**a**t.

These words begin with the short "a" sound. Fill in the letter **a** for that sound. Say the words. Circle the two animals.

<u>a</u>pple

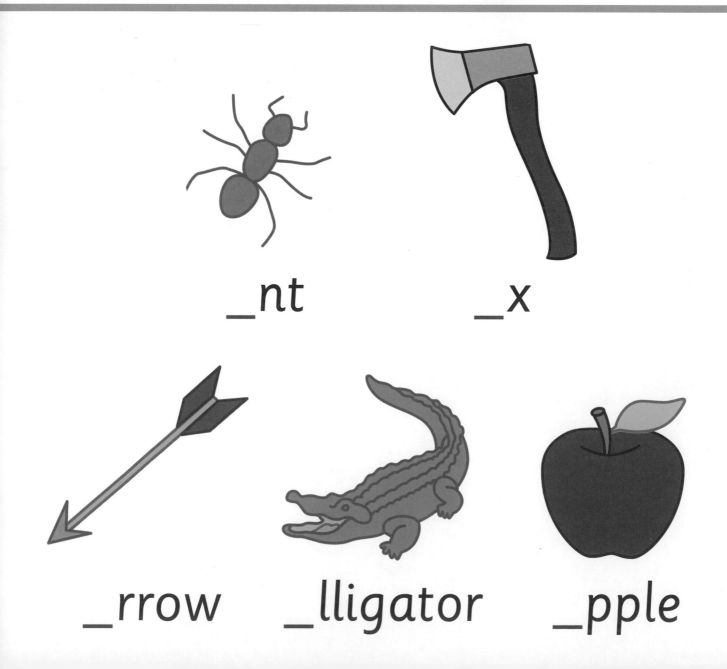

_nt

_x

_rrow

_lligator

_pple

Time Filler:
Try this action: act like an angry alligator and snap "a, a, a."

Add a letter from the alphabet to make a string of rhyming words:
a b c d e f g h i j k l m n o p q r s t u v w x y z

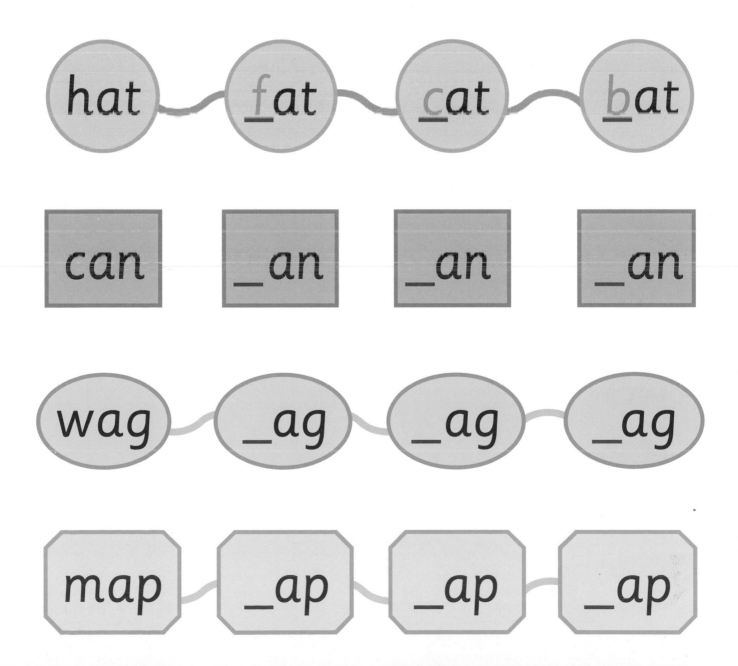

hat — _f_at — _c_at — _b_at

can — _an — _an — _an

wag — _ag — _ag — _ag

map — _ap — _ap — _ap

"b" Sound

Say "b" for **b**ig,
bouncy **b**alls
in a **bu**bbly tu**b**.

Add the letter **b** and say the
words. Listen to the "b" sound.
Connect each word to its picture.

<u>b</u>at

_at

_ell

_oat

_utton

_owl

Time Filler:
In 10 minutes, how many things can you find around your house that begin with the letter **b**?

Look at the picture. Draw a line from each question to its answer.

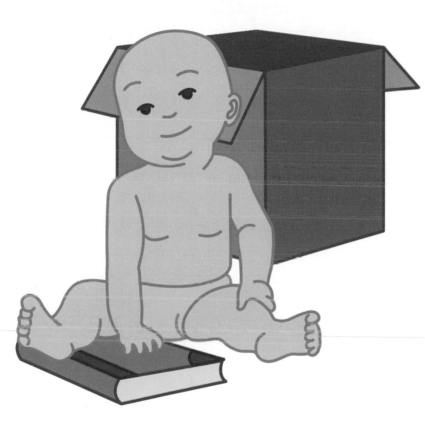

What is behind the baby?   box

What is below the baby?   ball

What is next to the baby?   book

What color is the book?   black

What color are the spots on the ball?   blue

"c" Sound

c and **k** both make the "c" sound. So does **ck**. Let's practice.

Write a **c** or **k** to complete these words. Make sure you use the right one. Say the words and listen to the "c" sound.

<u>c</u>ow   <u>k</u>ite

_ar   _ing   _oala

_ey   _andle   _ake

Time Filler:
Look around your house for objects with the "c" sound. Does the sound come at the beginning, in the middle, or at the end of the words?

Write the letters **ck** in the spaces to complete each word.

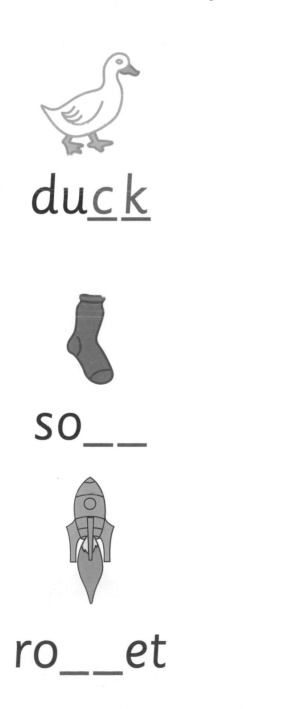

du<u>c</u>k

lo___

so___

clo___

ro___et

bu___le

"d" Sound

Say "d" for **dea**d**ly,** **d**angerous **d**inosaurs **d**oing a **d**ance.

These words begin with the "d" sound. Fill in the letter **d** and say the words.

 <u>d</u>iver

 __uck

 __octor

 __iver

 __og

 __ancer

 __entist

Time Filler:
Draw a duck diving,
a dog digging, and
a dancer.

Say the words. Circle the words that begin with the "d" sound.

(dolphin)   cloud   doll

Say the words. Circle the words that end with the "d" sound.

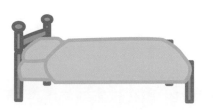

bed   dinosaur   hand

Short "e" Sound

The "e" sound can start words like **e**gg. It can also be in the middle of words like n**e**st.

All of these words begin with the short "e" sound.
Fill in the letter **e** for that sound. Say the words.

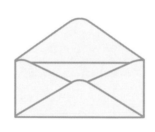

_egg

_nvelope

_lephant

Complete these signs with the capital letter **E**.
Listen to the words.

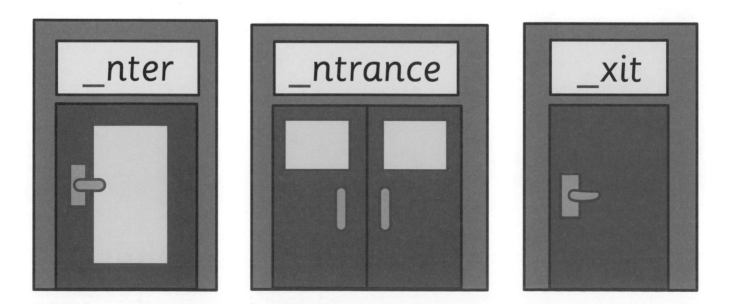

_nter   _ntrance   _xit

Time Filler:
Pretend to be an explorer on an exciting expedition in the jungle. What happens when you meet an elephant?

Add a letter from the alphabet to make a string of rhyming words:
a b c d e f g h i j k l m n o p q r s t u v w x y z

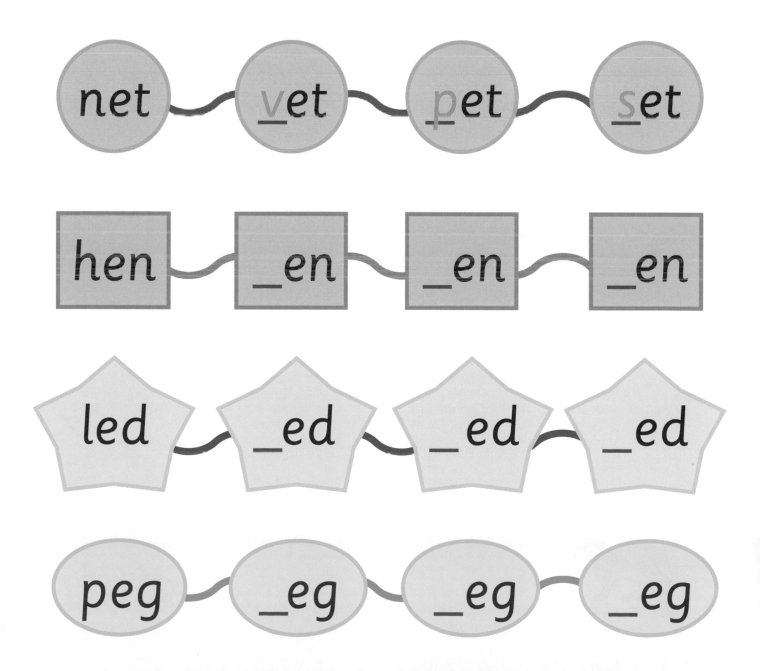

net — _vet — _pet — _set

hen — _en — _en — _en

led — _ed — _ed — _ed

peg — _eg — _eg — _eg

"f" Sound

Say "f" for a **f**ish **f**licks and **f**lashes its **f**ins swiftly.

Add the letter f and say the words. Listen to the "f" sound. Connect each word to its picture.

 <u>f</u>erret

 _erret

_ish

 _ox

 _eather

Time Filler:
Make a paper fan: First, fold over a top edge, then flip the paper and fold the edge over again. Keep flipping over and folding until you reach the final edge. Say flip and fold each time.

Throw a die. Move forward the number of spaces shown on the die. Say the name of the picture you land on aloud. Is the "f" sound at the beginning, in the middle, or at the end? Keep going until you pass the FINISH line.

"g" Sound

Gorillas **g**o "**G**lug, **g**lug, **g**lug!" when **g**ulping **g**allons of water.

These words begin with the "g" sound. Fill in the letter **g** for that sound. Say the words.

_gift

__oat

__ate

__ift

__oose

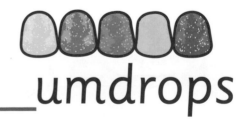

__umdrops

__uitar

Say the words. Circle the words that end with the "g" sound.

peg

dog

peg

rug

goose

pig

gate

"h" Sound

Say "h" for a **h**airy **h**amster **h**appy in the **h**ay.

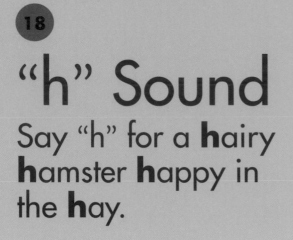

Circle the heaviest hen. Say "hen."

Circle the highest house. Say "house."

Circle the hottest hamburger. Say "hamburger."

Circle the huge helmet.
Say "helmet."

Complete the words with the letter **h**. Say the words and listen to the "h" sound. Draw a line from each word to its picture.

<u>h</u>air   _ay   _orse

_elmet   _and   _oof

Build the Words

Let us build some words
with the letter sounds
you have practiced.

**Make a word using the
letter tiles. Say the letter
sounds aloud and then say
the word. Write the word.**

h e n   _h _e _n_

① h e n _ _ _

② b a g _ _ _

③ f a n _ _ _

Time Filler:
Say three words that rhyme
with each of these words:
bag, cat, and hen.

④ d a d _ _ _

⑤ g e t _ _ _

⑥ c a p _ _ _

Short "i" Sound

The "i" sound can start words like **i**nsect. It can also be in the middle of words like s**i**t.

Say the words.
Circle the words that begin with the short "i" sound.

insect

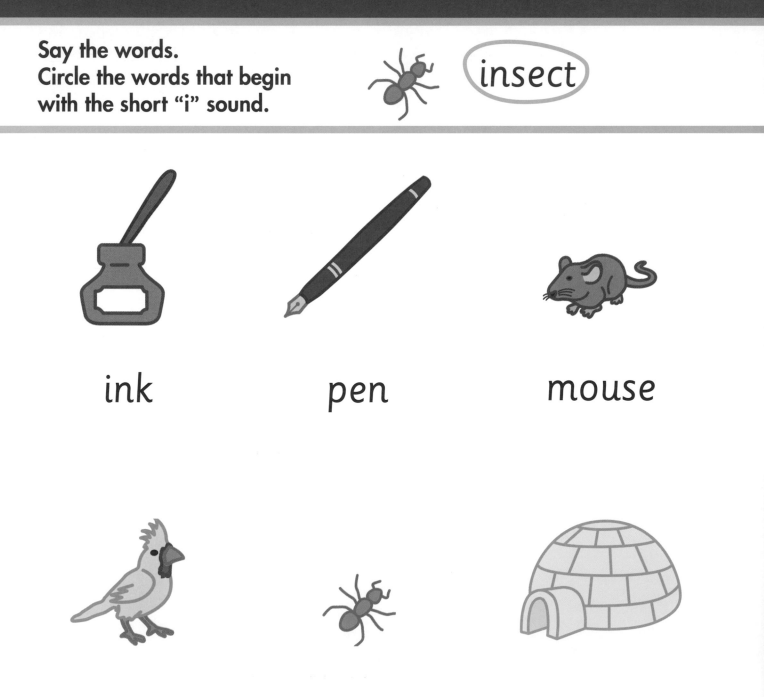

ink

pen

mouse

bird

insect

igloo

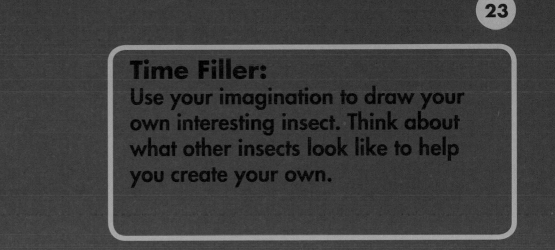

Time Filler:
Use your imagination to draw your own interesting insect. Think about what other insects look like to help you create your own.

Add a letter from the alphabet to make a string of rhyming words:

a b c d e f g h i j k l m n o p q r s t u v w x y z

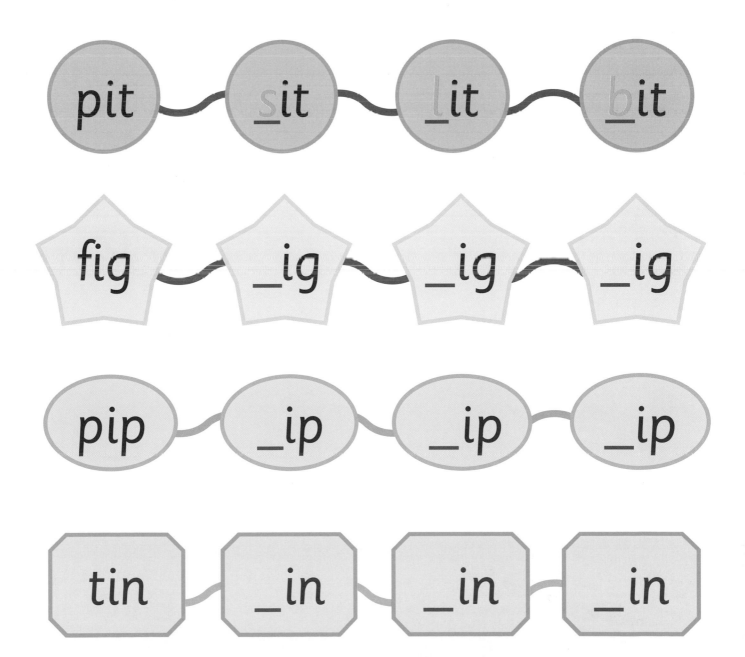

"j" Sound

Say "j" for **j**olly **j**umping
jack-in-the-box.

Add the letter **j** and say the words.
Listen to the "j" sound. Connect
each word to its picture.

_jewel

_ellyfish

_acket

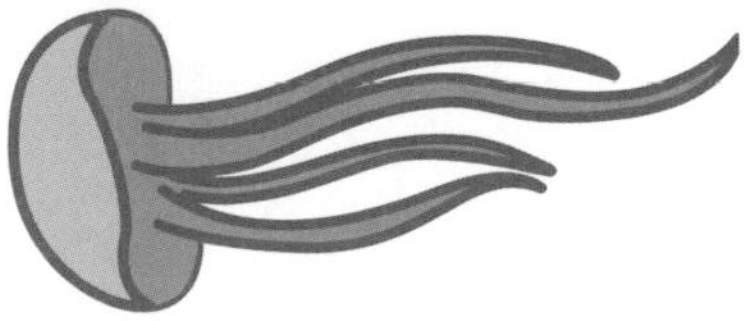

_et

_ewel

Time Filler:
Try these activities:
how many jumps can you do
in a minute? Jog in place for
a minute. Learn to juggle.

Complete these pictures.
Color the four balls for
the joker to juggle.

juggle

joker

jump

Color the hurdle
for the athlete
to jump over.

"l" Sound

Lick, **l**ick, **l**ick!
Lions **l**ove
lemon **l**o**ll**ipops.

Read the words in the ladders. Circle the words that begin with the letter l.

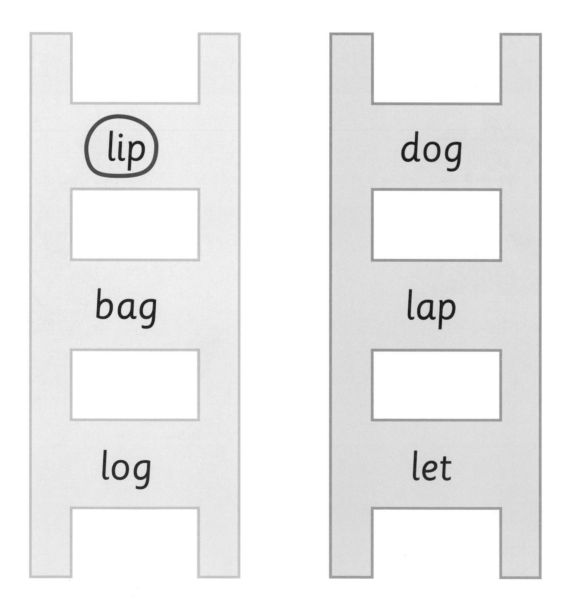

Time Filler:
Outside, collect 10 lovely leaves.
Look at them closely and say why
you like them.

Say the words. Circle the words that begin with the "l" sound.

(leaf)   bell   lamp

Say the words. Circle the words that end with the "l" sound.

snail   lion   bowl

"m" Sound

Say "m" for a
mouthful of **m**elting
marsh**m**allows. **Mmm**.

These words begin with the "m" sound.
Fill in the letter **m** and say the words.
Listen to the "m" sound.

 <u>m</u>oon

_op

_oon

_ap

_ug

_ouse

_onkey

Time Filler:
Try these activities:
march like a drummer, munch like a mischievous monkey, and make a medal.

Listen to the names of the months.
Circle the five months that have the "m" sound in them.

Months of the year	
January	July
February	August
(March)	September
April	October
May	November
June	December

"n" Sound

Say "n" for **n**oisy,
nosy **n**eighbors
ru**nn**ing **n**ext door.

Write the letter n in the space to complete each word.

n̲uts   _est

9
_i_e   _eck   _urse

Time Filler:
Use a newspaper or a magazine to find three pictures of things that begin with the "n" sound.

Add the letter **n** and say these number words. Listen to the "n" sound. Connect each number word to its number.

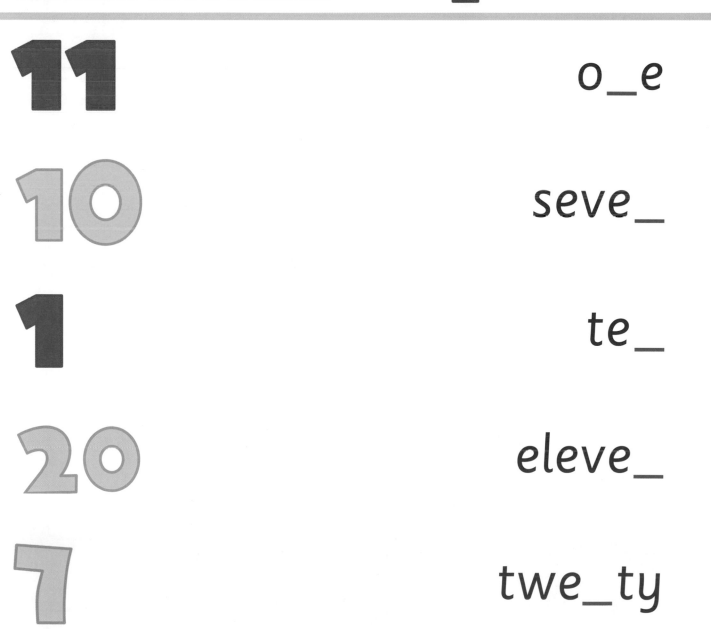

1 o<u>n</u>e

11

10

1

20

7

o_e

seve_

te_

eleve_

twe_ty

Short "o" Sound

The "o" sound can start words like **o**range, or be in the middle of words like lem**o**n.

Say the word for each picture.
Listen to the beginning sound.
Circle the picture that begins
with the short "o" sound.
Add the letter **o** to each word.

<u>o</u>x

_ctopus

_strich

_range

_x

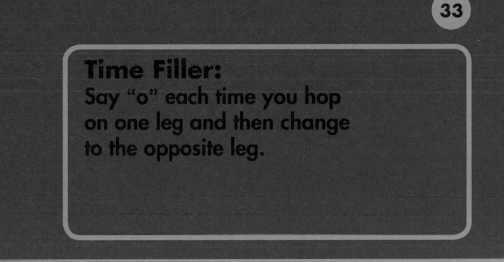

Add a letter from the alphabet to make a string of rhyming words:

a b c d e f g h i j k l m n o p q r s t u v w x y z

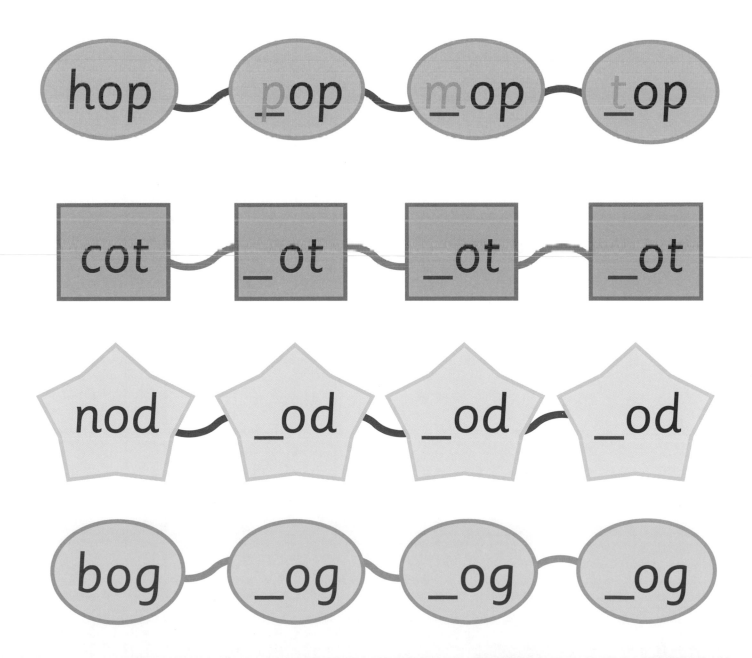

hop — pop — _op — _op

cot — _ot — _ot — _ot

nod — _od — _od — _od

bog — _og — _og — _og

"p" Sound

Say "p" for **p**ick a
petal from a po**pp**y.

Read the words in the ladders. Circle the words that begin with the letter p.

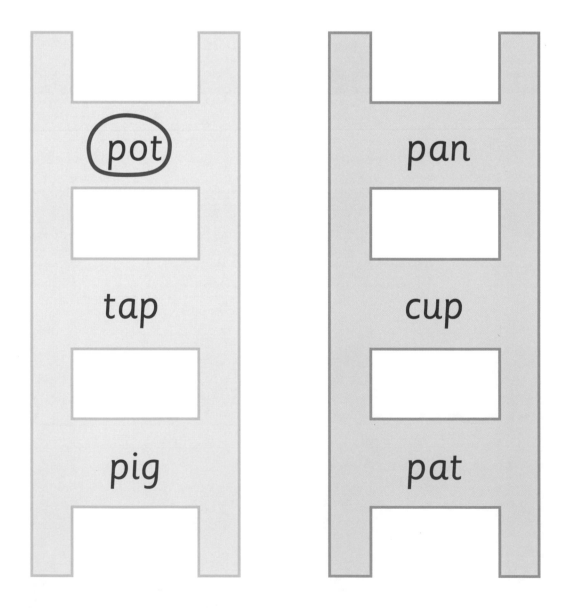

Time Filler:
Plan a pirate treasure map.
Put an X to mark the spot
where the treasure is.

Write the letter **p** in the space to complete each word.

peacock

_otato

_encil

_u__et

_enguin

"qu" Sound

The "qu" sound says "kw."
The letter **q** loves **u**, **q** does
not go anywhere without **u**.

Circle the four animals that move quickly.

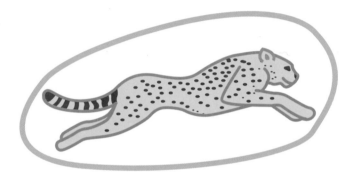

Time Filler:
How quickly can you say
the alphabet?
a, b, c, d, e, f, g, h, i, j, k, l, m,
n, o, p, q, r, s, t, u, v, w, x, y, z.
Now, say the alphabet quietly.

Circle the letters **qu** in each of the words. Then color the pictures.

quack

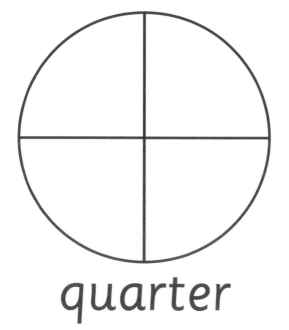

quarter

quilt

"r" Sound

Say "r" for **r**ascal **r**etriever being **r**ough with the **r**ug. **Rrr.**

Add the letter **r** and say the words. Listen to the "r" sound. Connect each word to its picture.

 _**r**_abbit

 _abbit

 _ing

_ocket

 _obot

 _ug

Where do you hear the "r" sound?
Say each word. Then circle the letter r in each word.

rope　　　door　　　jar

giraffe　　　chair　　　roof

Build the Words

Let us build some words
with the letter sounds
you have practiced.

Make a word using the letter tiles. Say the letter sounds aloud and then say the word. Write the word.

j o g j o g

① m o p _ _ _

② j o g _ _ _

③ p o t _ _ _

Time Filler:
Say three words that rhyme
with each of these words:
hot, log, and rip.

④ k i t _ _ _

⑤ r i p _ _ _

⑥ l i p _ _ _

"s" Sound

Say "s" for **s**unbathing on **s**oft **s**and and **s**wimming in the **s**ea.

These words begin with the "s" sound. Fill in the letter **s** for that sound. Say the words.

 <u>s</u>aw

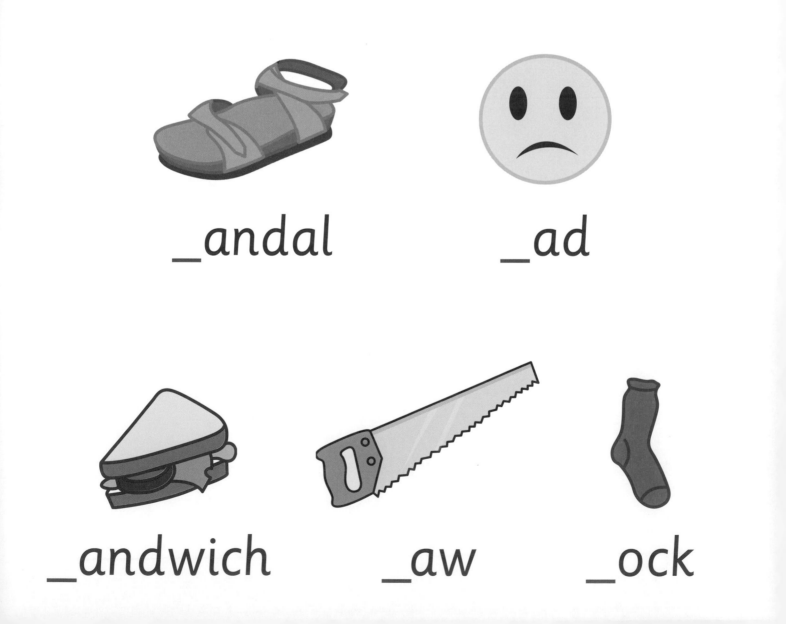

_andal

_ad

_andwich

_aw

_ock

Complete the words with the letter **s**. Say the words and listen to the "s" sound. Draw a line from each word to its picture.

s and   _ea   _un

_ky   _ungla__e_

"t" Sound

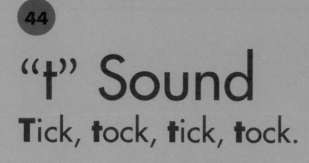

Tick, tock, tick, tock.

Read the words in the ladders. Circle the words that begin with the letter t.

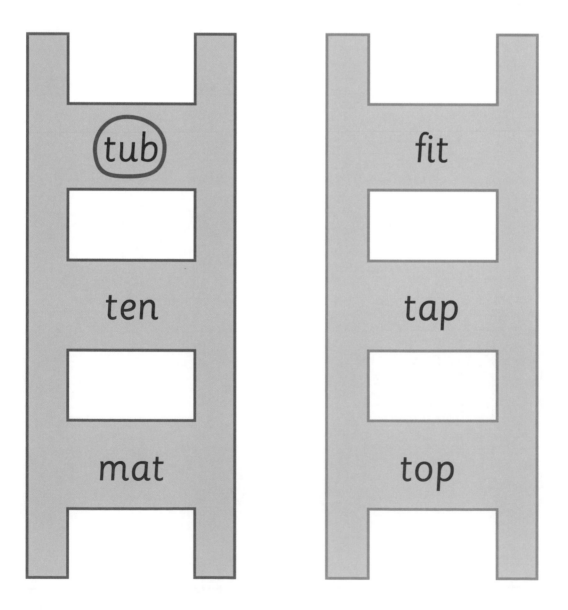

Time Filler:
Try saying this tongue twister:
ten terrible tigers tickled Tom twice.
Think of your own tongue twisters
for the "t" sound.

Write the letter **t** in the space to complete each word.

_t_ree

_ur_le

_able

_iger

_rain

_en_

Short "u" Sound

The "u" sound can start words like **u**mbrella, or be in the middle of words like s**u**n.

Say the words. Circle the words that begin with the "u" sound.

umbrella

duck

rug

under

nut

sun

bus

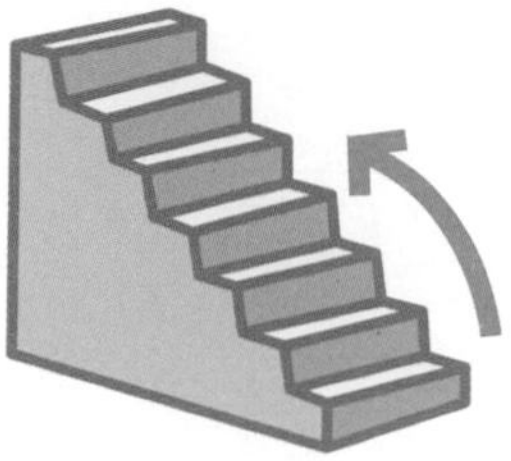

up

umbrella

truck

Time Filler:
Try these activities:
undo buttons, zip up
a jacket, and untie
shoelaces.

Add a letter from the alphabet to make a string of rhyming words:
a b c d e f g h i j k l m n o p q r s t u v w x y z

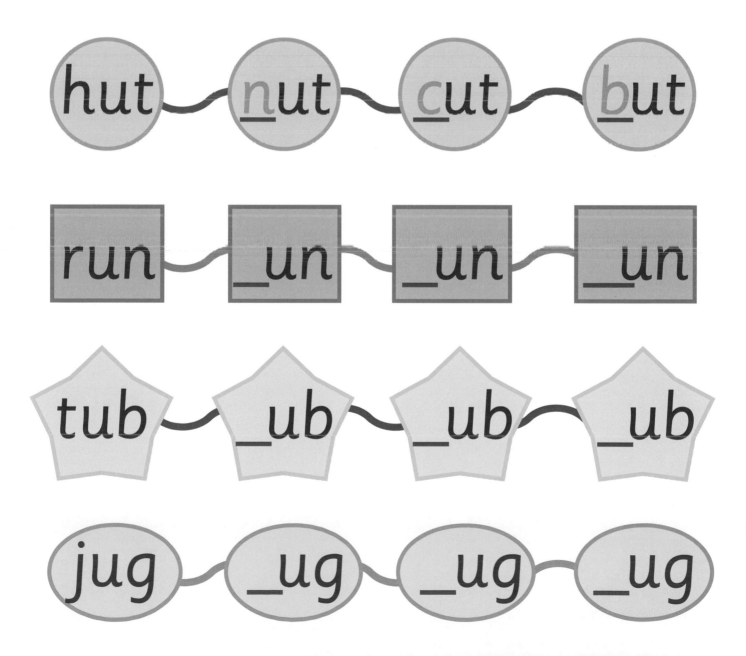

hut   _nut   _cut   _but

run   _un   _un   _un

tub   _ub   _ub   _ub

jug   _ug   _ug   _ug

"v" Sound

Say "v" for a **v**ase
of **v**elvet **v**iolets.

Add the letter **v** and say the
words. Listen to the "v" sound.
Connect each word to its picture.

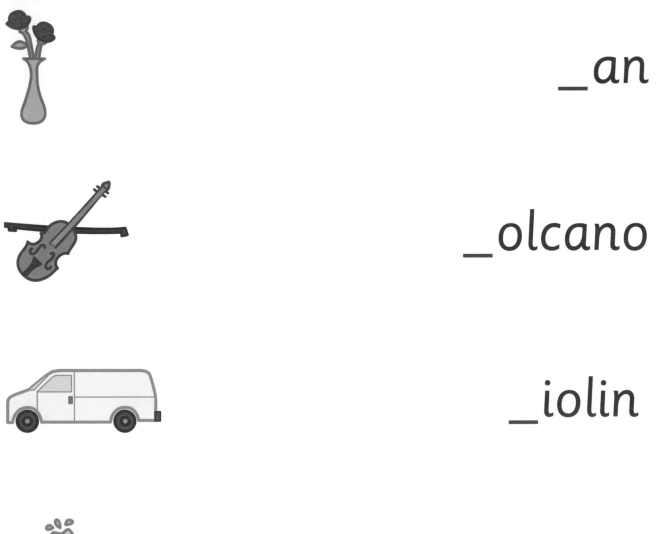

_v_an

_an

_olcano

_iolin

_ase

These words have the "v" sound in the middle or at the end. Fill in the letter **v** for that sound.

 do_v_e

 di_er

 se_en

 glo_e

 fi_e

 o_en

 do_e

 kni_es

 ri_er

ele_en

"w" Sound

Say "w" for **w**ash
and **w**ipe **w**indows
with **w**ater.

Say the word for each picture.
Listen to the beginning sound.
Circle the picture that begins
with the "w" sound.
Add the letter **w** to each word.

<u>w</u>indmill

 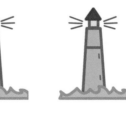 

_indmill

_indow

_itch

_orm

Complete the words with the letter **w**.
Say the words and listen to the "w" sound.
Draw a line from each word to its picture.

<u>w</u>ave

_ater

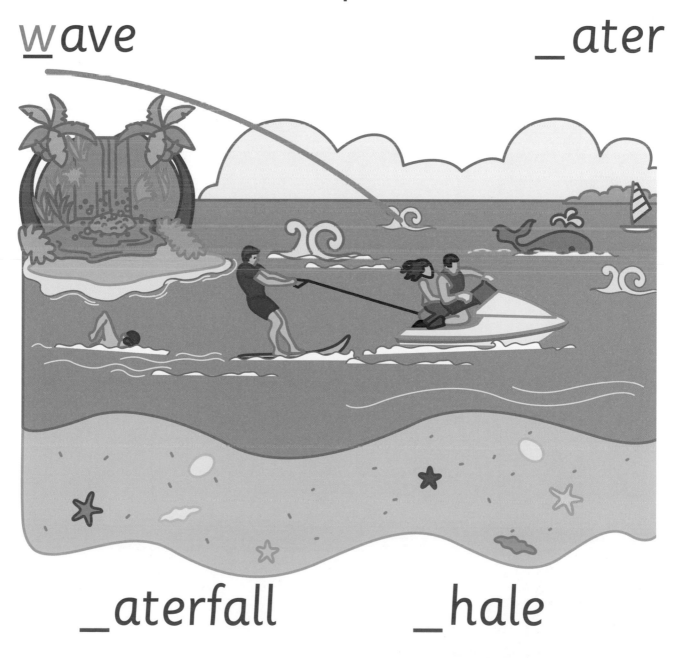

_aterfall

_hale

"x" Sound

Fi**x** a bo**x** for a fo**x**:
say the "x" sound
as "ks."

Add the letter **x** to complete each word.
Say the words. Listen to the "x" sound.
Connect each word to its picture.

6 ‿ si<u>x</u>

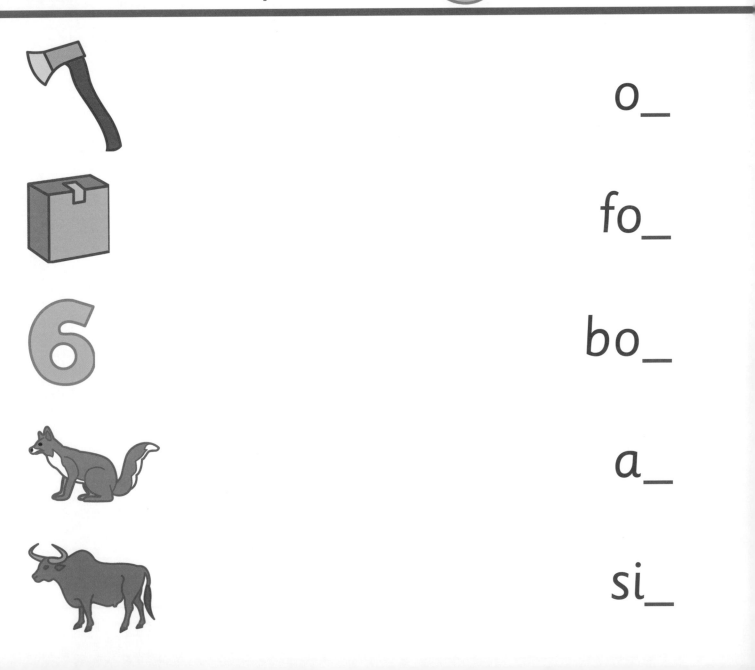

o_

fo_

bo_

a_

si_

Find the letter **x** in the words below.
Circle the letter in each word.

fox

ox

box

x-ray

"y" Sound

Say "y" for **y**anking,
yellow **y**o-**y**os.

Add the letter y to make the "y" sound. Connect each word to its picture.

 _yo-yo

 _o- _o

_awn

_ellow

 _arn

Time Filler:
Yell a happy "Yes!"
and a joyous "Yippee!"

Find the letter y in the words. Circle the letter y.

year   you   yes

A yacht is a kind of ship. Color the yacht.

"z" Sound

Say "z" for a **z**ebra's **z**any, **z**ippy stripes.

Say the words. Circle the words that begin with the "z" sound.

(zero)

zebra

bulldozer

zip

lizard

zoo

wizard

zig-zag

prize

zero

Time Filler:
Try these zappy moves between two points: zip across, zig-zag across, and zoom across.

Some sound-effect words use the "z" sound. Say these words below. Circle the letters that make the "z" sound.

"ch" Sound

Say "ch" for **ch**ewing and
crun**ch**ing on a mint-
chocolate **ch**ip cookie.

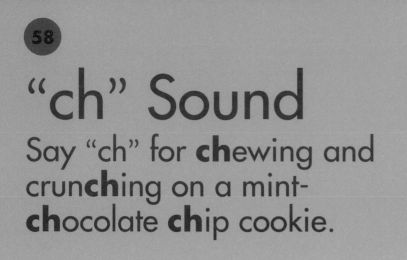

Add the letters **ch** and say the
words. Listen to the "ch" sound.
Connect each word to its picture.

__c__heese

__eetah

__eese

__icken

__ur__

__ocolate

Time Filler:
Try making these sounds: chirp like a grasshopper, cheep like a cheerful chick, chatter like a cheeky monkey, and chuckle like a chimpanzee.

Write the letters **ch** in the space to complete each word.

c h ick

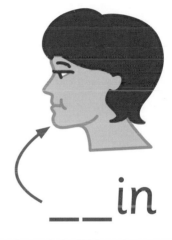

__in

__erry

__air

"sh" Sound

Say "sh" for **sh**ifting **sh**apes that **sh**iver and **sh**ake in the **sh**adows.

Say the words. Circle the words that begin with the "sh" sound.

(shell)

shark

shell

dish

fish

shape

ship

shoe

bush

shirt

Time Filler:
In 10 minutes, how many things can you find around your house with the "sh" sound in their names?

Say these words below.
Circle the letters that make the "sh" sound.

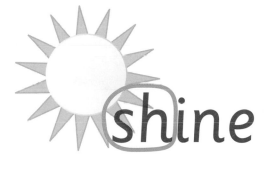

shine

shock

shrink

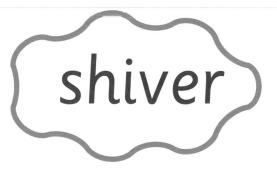

shiver

shake

"th" Sound

Say "th" for 33 **th**irsty **th**ieves **th**udding and **th**umping **th**rough the **th**understorm.

Add the letters **th** and say the words. Listen to the "th" sound. Connect each word to its picture.

<u>t h</u>umb

3

__umb

__ree

__rone

Time Filler:
Think of three thick things, three thin things, and three things you can throw.

Circle the thickest tree.

Circle the thickest brush.

Circle the thinnest book.

Circle the thinnest branch.

Build the Words

Let us build some words
with the letter sounds
you have practiced.

Make a word using the letter tiles. Say the letter sounds aloud and then say the word. Write the word.

y a m   y a m

(1) y a m   _ _ _

(2) w e t   _ _ _

(3) z i p   _ _ _

Time Filler:
Say three words that rhyme
with each of these words:
jug, hut, and yet.

4  t u b _ _ _

5  s u n _ _ _

6  v a n _ _ _

Answers:

4–5 Short "a" Sound

6–7 "b" Sound

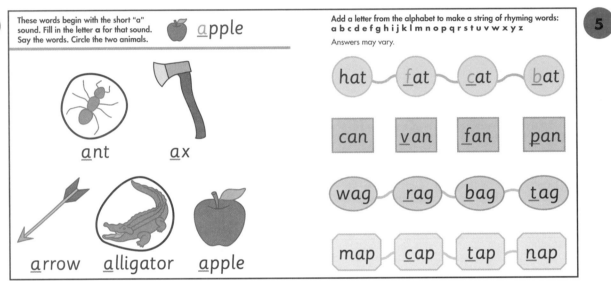

4 These words begin with the short "a" sound. Fill in the letter a for that sound. Say the words. Circle the two animals.

a̲pple

a̲nt a̲x

a̲rrow a̲lligator a̲pple

5 Add a letter from the alphabet to make a string of rhyming words:
a b c d e f g h i j k l m n o p q r s t u v w x y z

Answers may vary.

hat f̲at c̲at b̲at

can v̲an f̲an pan

wag r̲ag b̲ag t̲ag

map c̲ap t̲ap n̲ap

Phonics is the name of the relationship between letters and sounds. This system helps children to learn to read and to spell. The first steps are to isolate and say the first, middle, and final sounds of consonant-vowel-consonant words. Connecting a sound with movement is also a useful way of reinforcing the sound and getting children interested.

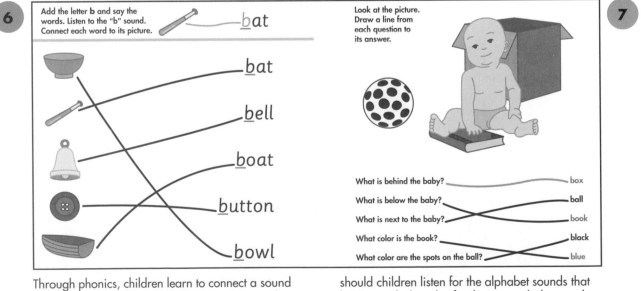

6 Add the letter b and say the words. Listen to the "b" sound. Connect each word to its picture.

b̲at

b̲at

b̲ell

b̲oat

b̲utton

b̲owl

7 Look at the picture. Draw a line from each question to its answer.

What is behind the baby? _____ box

What is below the baby? _____ ball

What is next to the baby? _____ book

What color is the book? _____ black

What color are the spots on the ball? _____ blue

Through phonics, children learn to connect a sound with a letter. They begin with the consonants and simple short vowels of the alphabet. Not only should children listen for the alphabet sounds that begin words, but also for those sounds that can be heard in the middle or ends of words.

Answers:

8–9 "c" Sound

10–11 "d" Sound

8 Write a **c** or **k** to complete these words. Make sure you use the right one. Say the words and listen to the "c" sound.

<u>c</u>ow   <u>k</u>ite

<u>c</u>ar   <u>k</u>ing   <u>k</u>oala

<u>k</u>ey   <u>c</u>andle   <u>c</u>ake

9 Write the letters **ck** in the spaces to complete each word.

du<u>ck</u>   lo<u>ck</u>

so<u>ck</u>   clo<u>ck</u>

ro<u>ck</u>et   bu<u>ck</u>le

The "c" sound is a little trickier as two letters of the alphabet make this same sound: the letter **c** and the letter **k**. Also the letters **ck** join together to make this same sound often at the ends of words. Two letters together making one sound are called digraphs. Further work on these pairings is covered in 1st Grade.

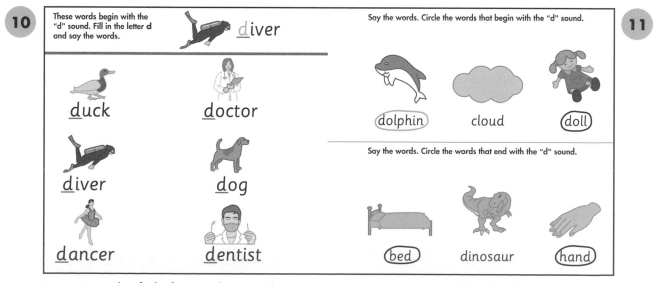

10 These words begin with the "d" sound. Fill in the letter **d** and say the words.

<u>d</u>iver

<u>d</u>uck   <u>d</u>octor

<u>d</u>iver   <u>d</u>og

<u>d</u>ancer   <u>d</u>entist

11 Say the words. Circle the words that begin with the "d" sound.

(dolphin)   cloud   (doll)

Say the words. Circle the words that end with the "d" sound.

(bed)   dinosaur   (hand)

It is easier to identify the first sound in a word, so focusing on first sounds can encourage children.

Keep praising your child as he/she works through these activities.

Answers:

12–13 Short "e" Sound
14–15 "f" Sound

 12 All of these words begin with the short "e" sound. Fill in the letter e for that sound. Say the words.

<u>e</u>gg   <u>e</u>nvelope   <u>e</u>lephant

Complete these signs with the capital letter **E**. Listen to the words.

Enter   Entrance   Exit

13 Add a letter from the alphabet to make a string of rhyming words:
a b c d e f g h i j k l m n o p q r s t u v w x y z
Answers may vary.

net — <u>v</u>et — <u>p</u>et — <u>s</u>et

hen — <u>p</u>en — <u>d</u>en — ten

led — <u>r</u>ed — <u>w</u>ed — <u>b</u>ed

peg — <u>l</u>eg — <u>k</u>eg — <u>b</u>eg

When you are out and about with children, point out letters on the printed signs around them. Sound out the first letter sound with them so that they continue to make a connection between sounds and letters. Also encourage children to spot certain letters in the words, or on car license plates.

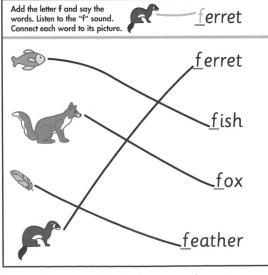 **14** Add the letter f and say the words. Listen to the "f" sound. Connect each word to its picture.

<u>f</u>erret

<u>f</u>erret

<u>f</u>ish

<u>f</u>ox

<u>f</u>eather

15 Throw a die. Move forward the number of spaces shown on the die. Say the name of the picture you land on aloud. Is the "f" sound at the beginning, in the middle, or at the end? Keep going until you pass the FINISH line.

Saying the names of animals is a good exercise for listening for the sounds of letters in the first, middle, and end positions. Playing games is another way of engaging children in the fun of phonics. "I Spy" is a classic game, but make sure that the alphabet sounds are used rather than the letter names, such as "f" instead of "eff."

Answers:

16–17 "g" Sound
18–19 "h" Sound

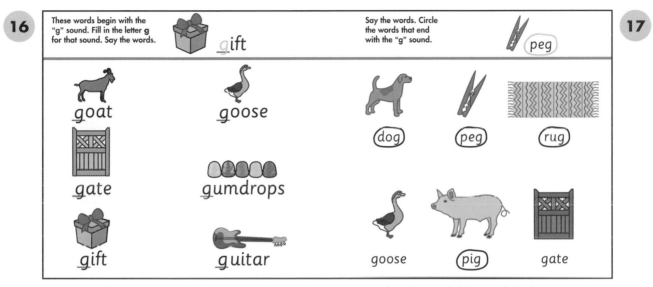

Naming and recognizing colors, instruments, animals, and other familiar objects is an excellent way to familiarize children with the beginning letter sounds and the corresponding letter.

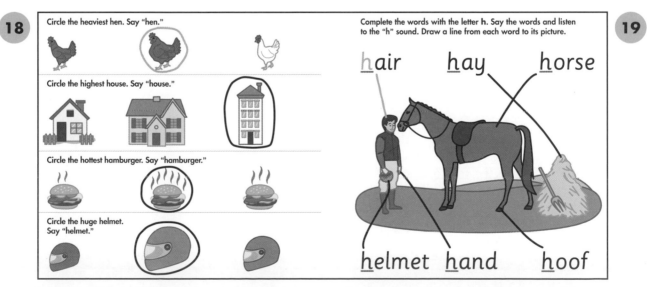

When saying letter sounds, make sure these do not have additional letters added to the sound, such as "huh" instead of the true short "h" on the breath.

For the accurate sound, separate the sounds in words, such as "hot," and keep the sounds light and short.

70

Answers:

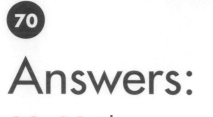

22–23 Short "i" Sound
24–25 "j" Sound

22 Say the words.
Circle the words that begin with the short "i" sound. (insect)

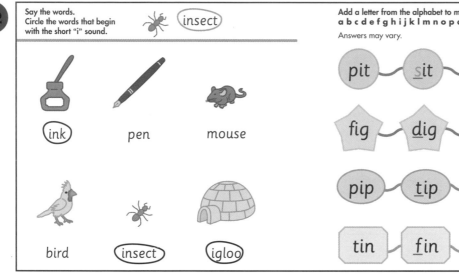

(ink)   pen   mouse

bird   (insect)   (igloo)

Children will be able to recognize and produce rhyming words by adding or substituting individual sounds in simple words to make new words. Encourage your child to work through the alphabet

23 Add a letter from the alphabet to make a string of rhyming words:
a b c d e f g h i j k l m n o p q r s t u v w x y z
Answers may vary.

pit — sit — lit — bit

fig — dig — pig — big

pip — tip — dip — lip

tin — fin — bin — pin

replacing the first letter in the rhyming string of words. Let them enjoy making nonsense words, although ask that they only write down actual words.

24 Add the letter **j** and say the words. Listen to the "j" sound. Connect each word to its picture. jewel

jellyfish

jacket

jet

jewel

Continue to support your child through the reading of the introductions, instructions, and saying the words on these activity pages. Encourage children

25 Complete these pictures. Color the four balls for the joker to juggle.

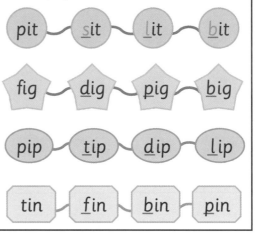

juggle

joker

jump

Color the hurdle for the athlete to jump over.

to say the letter sounds while they write the letter and as they jump and jog. Phonics can be made fun through activities that link the saying and doing.

Answers:

26–27 "l" Sound
28–29 "m" Sound

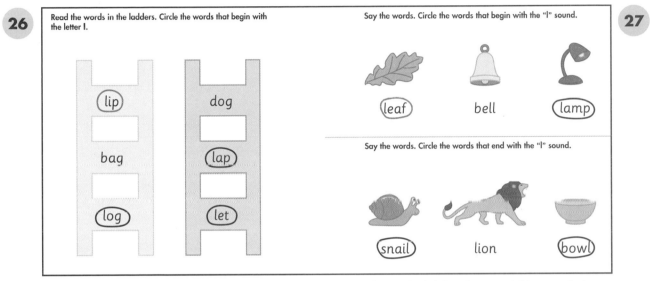

26 Read the words in the ladders. Circle the words that begin with the letter **l**.

Say the words. Circle the words that begin with the "l" sound. **27**

Say the words. Circle the words that end with the "l" sound.

Activities in this book encourage children both to start reading words with three simple letter sounds and to use the pictures to say the words aloud, listening for where the letter sounds appear in words. On the left hand page, children work down each ladder and spot the words that begin with the "l" sound. Help your child say the words in the same way as on the blue Build the Words pages.

28 These words begin with the "m" sound. Fill in the letter **m** and say the words. Listen to the "m" sound.

Listen to the names of the months. Circle the five months that have the "m" sound in them. **29**

When introducing the "m" sound, be careful to say "mmm" rather than "muh." These pages continue to encourage children to listen out for a specific consonant sound both at the beginning and in the middle of words and to reinforce through actions. For further activity, look through the letter **m** section of a simple children's dictionary to find these and other words beginning with **m**.

Answers:

30–31 "n" Sound
32–33 Short "o" Sound

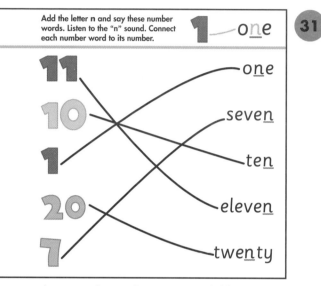

30 Write the letter **n** in the space to complete each word.

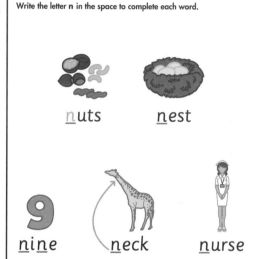

<u>n</u>uts   <u>n</u>est

<u>n</u>ine   <u>n</u>eck   <u>n</u>urse

31 Add the letter **n** and say these number words. Listen to the "n" sound. Connect each number word to its number.

1 — o<u>n</u>e

11
10
1
20
7

o<u>n</u>e
seve<u>n</u>
te<u>n</u>
eleve<u>n</u>
twe<u>n</u>ty

Children will become increasingly familiar with numbers and their corresponding written names. Early in math, children learn to read and recognize written number words, and practice writing them.

As they write the words, encourage children to say the word aloud so as to reinforce the sounds and the action of writing the letters.

32 Say the word for each picture. Listen to the beginning sound. Circle the picture that begins with the short "o" sound. Add the letter **o** to each word.

<u>o</u>x

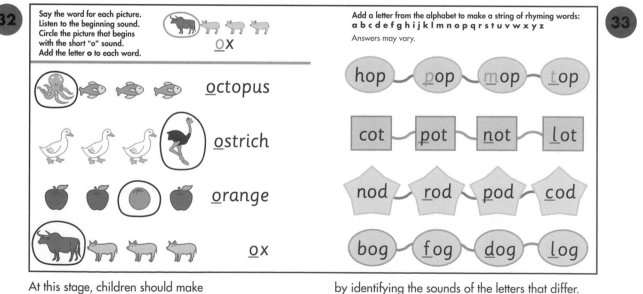

<u>o</u>ctopus

<u>o</u>strich

<u>o</u>range

<u>o</u>x

33 Add a letter from the alphabet to make a string of rhyming words: a b c d e f g h i j k l m n o p q r s t u v w x y z

Answers may vary.

hop — <u>p</u>op — <u>m</u>op — <u>t</u>op

cot — <u>p</u>ot — <u>n</u>ot — <u>l</u>ot

nod — <u>r</u>od — <u>p</u>od — <u>c</u>od

bog — <u>f</u>og — <u>d</u>og — <u>l</u>og

At this stage, children should make the connection that words when written are made by a specific sequence of letters. The rhyming word activity helps children to distinguish between similarly spelled words

by identifying the sounds of the letters that differ. Reading poetry or singing songs supports children's awareness of words that rhyme and rhyming letter patterns.

Answers:

34–35 "p" Sound
36–37 "qu" Sound

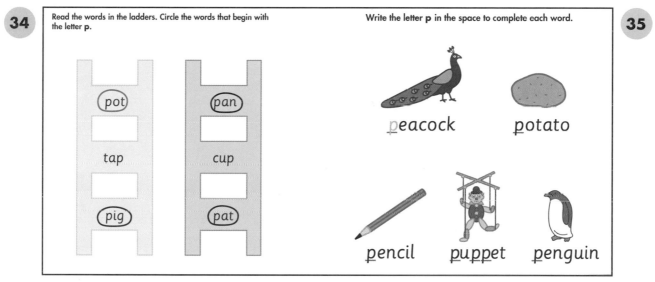

34 Read the words in the ladders. Circle the words that begin with the letter **p**.

pot
pan
tap
cup
pig
pat

35 Write the letter **p** in the space to complete each word.

peacock   potato

pencil   puppet   penguin

As children work down each ladder, ask them to say whether the letter **p** is the first, middle or last sound in each word. For further interest, point out that the

"p" sound in the middle of puppet is made by doubling the **p**. This happens when there is a short vowel sound just before.

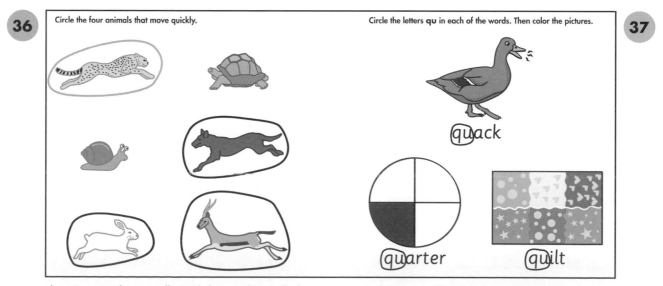

36 Circle the four animals that move quickly.

37 Circle the letters **qu** in each of the words. Then color the pictures.

quack

quarter   quilt

The "qu" sound is actually said "kw" and is spelled with the digraph **qu**. This is one of the trickier letter sounds for children to grasp. Children need to know the order of the letters in the alphabet to help with further language arts skills, such as finding words

in a dictionary. The alphabet is often said or sung using the letters' names. Explain to children that letters have names as well as sounds and they need to learn both.

Answers:

38–39 "r" Sound
42–43 "s" Sound

38 Add the letter **r** and say the words. Listen to the "r" sound. Connect each word to its picture.

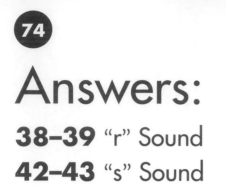

<u>r</u>abbit

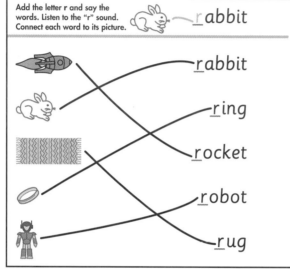

<u>r</u>abbit

<u>r</u>ing

<u>r</u>ocket

<u>r</u>obot

<u>r</u>ug

For the "r" sound say "rrr" rather than "ruh," and encourage children to say the sound as they roar around for the time filler. Circling the letter in the

39 Where do you hear the "r" sound? Say each word. Then circle the letter **r** in each word.

(r)ope   doo(r)   ja(r)

gi(r)affe   chai(r)   (r)oof

word helps children learn about the relationship between the different letters in a word.

42 These words begin with the "s" sound. Fill in the letter **s** for that sound. Say the words.

 <u>s</u>aw

<u>s</u>andal   <u>s</u>ad

<u>s</u>andwich   <u>s</u>aw   <u>s</u>ock

The letter **s** is often found as part of letter sound blends, such as **sp**, **sl**, **st**, **sk**, and **sn**. Encourage children to say these letter sounds separately and then blend them together. A further activity is to

43 Complete the words with the letter **s**. Say the words and listen to the "s" sound. Draw a line from each word to its picture.

<u>s</u>and   <u>s</u>ea   <u>s</u>un

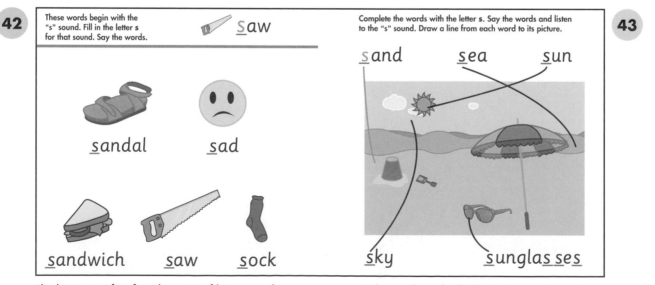

<u>s</u>ky   sunglas<u>s</u>es

count the number of syllables in the words on this page, by saying the words broken into segments. Words such as "san-dal" and "sand-wich" each have two syllables.

Answers:

44–45 "t" Sound

46–47 Short "u" Sound

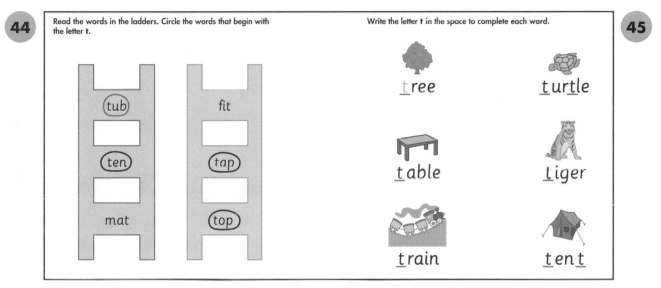

44 Read the words in the ladders. Circle the words that begin with the letter t.

tub

ten

mat

fit

tap

top

45 Write the letter t in the space to complete each word.

t ree

t able

t rain

t urtle

t iger

t en t

Enjoy learning and saying tongue twisters together. Explain to children that they are tricky because the same first letter sound is used many times and

requires the lips to move with smoothness and dexterity. They also help to improve the quality and clarity of speech.

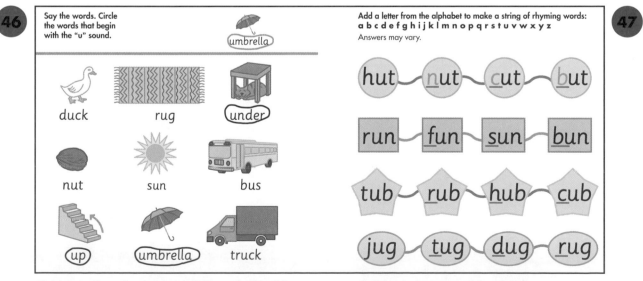

46 Say the words. Circle the words that begin with the "u" sound.

umbrella

duck

rug

under

nut

sun

bus

up

umbrella

truck

47 Add a letter from the alphabet to make a string of rhyming words:
a b c d e f g h i j k l m n o p q r s t u v w x y z
Answers may vary.

hut — nut — cut — but

run — fun — sun — bun

tub — rub — hub — cub

jug — tug — dug — rug

Children will need to listen carefully to identify if the short "u" sound is coming at the beginning or the middle of the words on page 46. As for the other red pages in this workbook, encourage children to

work through the letters of the alphabet to make rhyming words, deciding if they have made nonsense or real words.

Answers:

48–49 "v" Sound
50–51 "w" Sound

48

Add the letter **v** and say the words. Listen to the "v" sound. Connect each word to its picture.

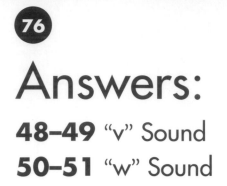

_v an

_v an

_v olcano

_v iolin

_v ase

As children reach the last handful of letters of the alphabet, the letter sounds become trickier. On these pages, encourage children to say the sounds

49

These words have the "v" sound in the middle or at the end. Fill in the letter **v** for that sound.

do_v e

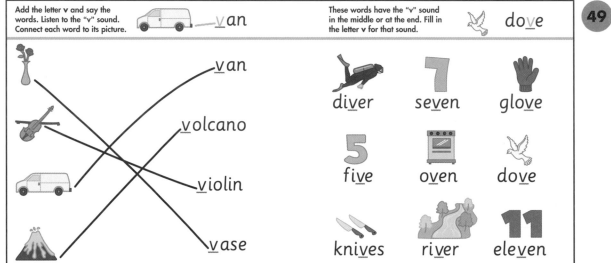

di_v er   se_v en   glo_v e

fi_v e   o_v en   do_v e

kni_v es   ri_v er   ele_v en

as they write the letters and as they act out driving vehicles. Avoid saying "vuh" as the sound is a reverberating "vvv."

50

Say the word for each picture. Listen to the beginning sound. Circle the picture that begins with the "w" sound. Add the letter **w** to each word.

_w indmill

_w indmill

_w indow

_w itch

_w orm

Continue to discuss with children the letter sounds they can see and hear around them. For the activities on these pages, encourage children

51

Complete the words with the letter **w**. Say the words and listen to the "w" sound. Draw a line from each word to its picture.

_w ave   _w ater

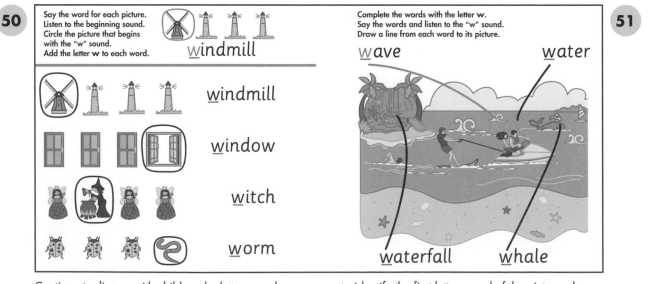

_w aterfall   _w hale

to identify the first letter sound of the pictures they have circled and what else they can see in the beach picture.

Answers:

52–53 "x" Sound

54–55 "y" Sound

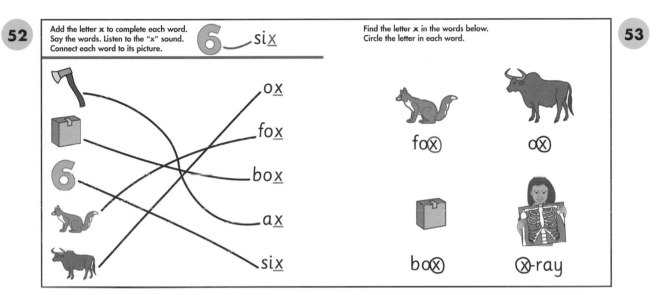

52 Add the letter **x** to complete each word. Say the words. Listen to the "x" sound. Connect each word to its picture.

6̶ si**x**

o**x**

fo**x**

bo**x**

a**x**

si**x**

Not many words begin with the letter **x** but a handful end in this letter. The sound is "ks," which is why many of these words rhyme with

53 Find the letter **x** in the words below. Circle the letter in each word.

fo⊗

o⊗

bo⊗

⊗-ray

plural nouns and verbs ending in **cks**, such as "licks," "clocks," and "sacks."

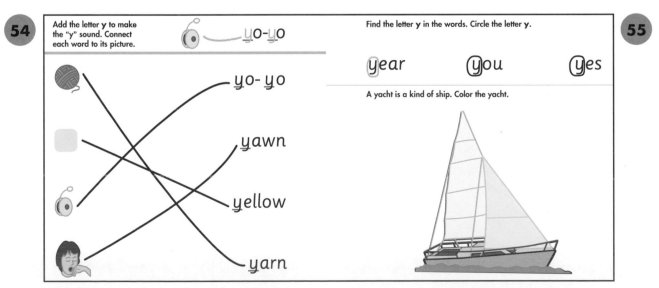

54 Add the letter **y** to make the "y" sound. Connect each word to its picture.

yo-**y**o

yo-**y**o

yawn

yellow

yarn

Once children have written the letter **y**, encourage them to repeat the words as the "y" sound can be tricky. What also makes things harder is finding that the letter **y** makes other sounds when it appears in words. Children will learn about this

55 Find the letter **y** in the words. Circle the letter **y**.

⑨ear   ⑨ou   ⑨es

A yacht is a kind of ship. Color the yacht.

over the next few grades, but they could notice that the **y** in "happy" makes an "ee" sound and the **y** in "joyous" is combined to make an "oy" sound.

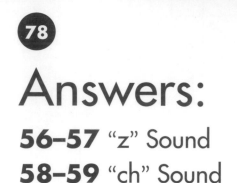

Answers:

56–57 "z" Sound
58–59 "ch" Sound

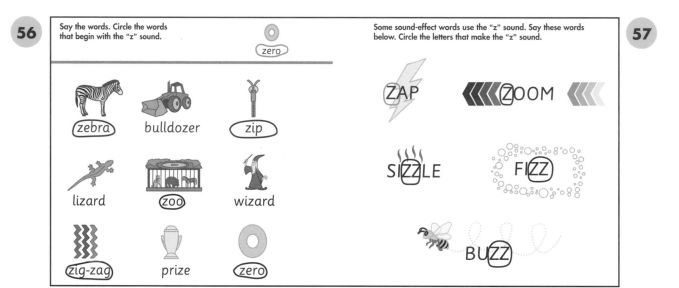

56 Say the words. Circle the words that begin with the "z" sound.

zero

zebra   bulldozer   zip

lizard   ZOO   wizard

zig-zag   prize   zero

57 Some sound-effect words use the "z" sound. Say these words below. Circle the letters that make the "z" sound.

ZAP   ZOOM

SIZZLE   FIZZ

BUZZ

For the sound effects, children will notice that when the letter **z** is doubled the two letters make the one "z" sound. Make sure that children circle both the letters together. Children may wish to draw their own patterns to describe these and other sound effects. Encourage children to know how to write and recognize letters in both upper-case and lower-case forms.

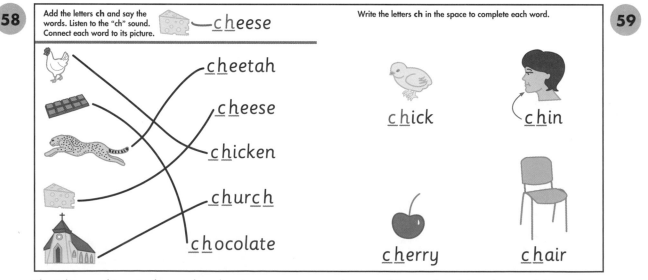

58 Add the letters **ch** and say the words. Listen to the "ch" sound. Connect each word to its picture.

cheese

cheetah

cheese

chicken

church

chocolate

59 Write the letters **ch** in the space to complete each word.

chick   chin

cherry   chair

The "ch" sound is a single sound made using two letters, which are called digraphs. It is important that children can say and hear the difference between this sound and the "sh" sound. It may help to explain that "ch" appears in the "choo-choo" noise of a train.

Answers:

60–61 "sh" Sound
62–63 "th" Sound

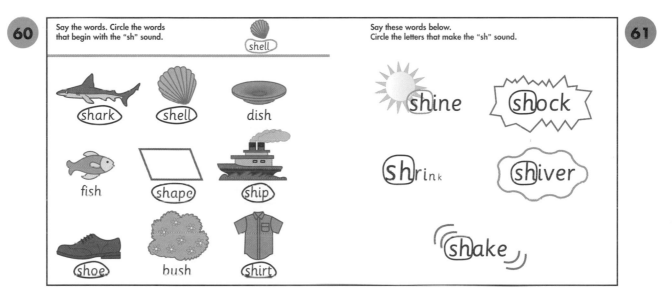

The "sh" sound made using the letters **sh** often appears in words so children should find plenty of objects with this sound as they look around their home. A useful action to learn the sound is to put a finger against the lips and say "shhh," meaning to be quiet.

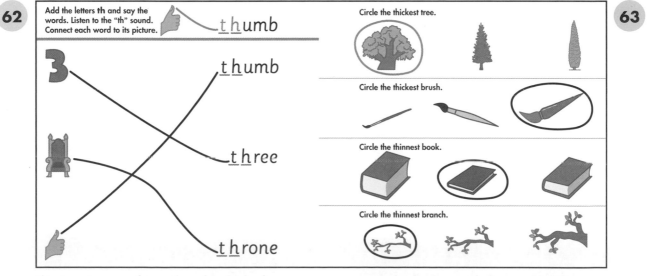

Phonics is just one of a number of methods of supporting children to read and write. This should be part of providing children with a range of reading material that helps them to read fluently, expressively, develop vocabulary, and build understanding of the meaning of words and text. Also encourage children to write creatively, using their imagination, or about topics that interest them.

Answers:

20–21 Build the Words
40–41 Build the Words
64–65 Build the Words

Systematic phonics practice helps children's word recognition, spelling, and reading comprehension. These "Build the Words" pages support the teaching of saying the separated letter sounds and then blending them together to form consonant-vowel-consonant words. At this stage, children practice spelling and writing one syllable words. For writing the words, make sure that children have a good pencil hold and sit correctly with their spare hand holding the book. The time filler activity can be extended by encouraging children to think of rhyming words to go with other words on these pages.

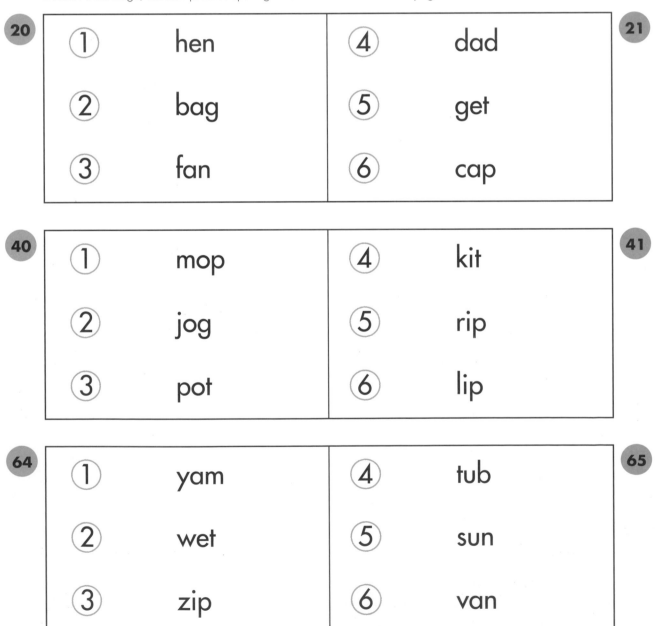

20
① hen
② bag
③ fan

21
④ dad
⑤ get
⑥ cap

40
① mop
② jog
③ pot

41
④ kit
⑤ rip
⑥ lip

64
① yam
② wet
③ zip

65
④ tub
⑤ sun
⑥ van